THE LIVING FESTIVALS

Jack Priestley — Series Editor

Easter

NORMA FAIRBAIRN and JACK PRIESTLEY

RELIGIOUS AND MORAL EDUCATION PRESS
An Imprint of Arnold-Wheaton

Religious and Moral Education Press
An Imprint of Arnold-Wheaton
Hennock Road, Exeter EX2 8RP

Pergamon Press Ltd
Headington Hill Hall, Oxford OX3 0BW

Pergamon Press Inc.
Maxwell House, Fairview Park, Elmsford, New York 10523

Pergamon Press Canada Ltd
Suite 104, 150 Consumers Road, Willowdale, Ontario M2J 1P9

Pergamon Press (Australia) Pty Ltd
P.O. Box 544, Potts Point, N.S.W. 2011

Pergamon Press GmbH
Hammerweg 6, D-6242 Kronberg, Federal Republic of Germany

Copyright © 1982 Norma Fairbairn and Jack Priestley

All rights reserved. No part of this publication may be reproduced, stored in a retrieval system, or transmitted, in any form or by any means, electronic, electrostatic, magnetic tape, mechanical, photocopying, recording or otherwise, without permission in writing from the publishers.

First published 1982

Reprinted 1983

Printed in Great Britain by A. Wheaton & Co. Ltd, Exeter

ISBN 0 08-027871-X non net
     0 08-027872-8 net

ACKNOWLEDGEMENTS

The authors and publisher wish to thank the following individuals and organizations who kindly provided photographs: Camera Press Ltd; Mary Evans Picture Library; Brian Shuel.

Cover photograph by courtesy of Picturepoint Ltd

Contents

Introduction — 5

1 Easter Celebrations — 7

2 Stories at Easter — 17

3 Symbols of Easter — 22

4 The Meaning of Easter — 27

Things to Do — 30

Material for Teachers — 32

Russian Christians celebrate Easter

Introduction

Easter is all about new life. It comes at a time when spring is in the air. It is a festival about hope for the future. There is nothing sad about Easter. All that is in the past. Winter has gone. The dark days are over; there are signs of new life everywhere.

For one group of people it is a festival above all other festivals. Every Sunday of the year Christians remember the Resurrection — the coming back to life of Jesus Christ. Easter day, for Christians, is like all the Sundays of the year rolled into one. It comes two days after Good Friday, when Jesus was crucified, but Good Friday and Easter are as far apart as darkness and light. For Christians, Easter is when sadness is suddenly turned into happiness, when despair turns into joy, when that which seemed dead is suddenly alive again, and is alive for evermore. Easter is a festival about the future, about believing in tomorrow.

On Easter day Christian churches all over the world are full of colour and flowers. The services are full of joyful singing. Everywhere there are symbols of light and laughter. The words heard most frequently are 'Christ is risen, Alleluia!'.

1

Easter Celebrations

Easter really begins at 6 p.m. on the Saturday. That is the day known as Easter Eve. It was at that time that the Jewish Sabbath came to an end, and we shall see in the next chapter why that was important for Easter.

The Saturday makes a complete break between Good Friday and Easter day. They are two quite different occasions and should not be mixed up. Not long ago it was customary for banks, shops, offices and factories to close on the Friday, open again for work on Saturday morning and then close again until Tuesday. Nowadays for many people it has become one continuous holiday but this book is only about Easter. (There is another book in this series which deals with the events of the week up to Good Friday.)

Easter is celebrated in many different ways all over the world. The celebrations are a mixture of religious services and all sorts of other activities, some of them quite crazy although we can give only a very few examples here. There are many more which it would be fun to find out about, especially the ones which happen near where you live.

There are three days of Easter festivities, Easter Eve, Easter day and Easter Monday, and we can divide the celebrations up like that, although some of them go on for more than one day. There are things that happen on Easter Tuesday as well, like the two-hundred-year-old custom of giving out large buns known as 'twopenny starvers' to the choir boys of St Michael's Church, Bristol.

Easter Eve

In many parts of the world Easter Eve is a day of getting ready. It is a day of cooking and washing and decorating. A lot goes on unnoticed and, particularly, inside churches there is a rush of activity. On Good Friday at the end of forty days of Lent, the churches are dark and depressing. They are often draped in black and purple and all the ornaments have been removed or covered. On Easter Eve it is all transformed; silver and gold colours appear everywhere — on the altar; the Bible markers; the pulpit cloth; and the priests' clothes, or vestments. The ornaments are brought back and masses of spring flowers decorate every corner.

In some homes, too, a great deal of work goes on, often in the kitchen. Special foods are got ready. It is traditional to eat roast lamb on Easter day but in many parts of the world it is accompanied by all sorts of other foods which also have to be prepared.

It is getting the Easter eggs ready which is the most common custom in many homes on Easter Eve. But in some parts of the world this is an operation which has already been going on for weeks. In Eastern Europe, in particular, decorating eggs is a work of art. The most detailed patterns are worked on to them, often with paint but sometimes with wax and dye.

In Poland Easter eggs, called *pisanki,* are real hens' eggs which have been 'blown' by piercing them with a needle at each end and then carefully blowing out the contents. A wax pattern is then made with the needle. The eggshell is dipped in dye which colours all the surface except where there is wax. This can be repeated with different colours, and in this way fine patterns are built up. By Easter Eve the finishing touches are being made and, with a coat of varnish added, they are ready to give away next morning. Some of these eggs last for years and years and have become family heirlooms.

The same sort of loving care goes into decorating eggs in other countries such as Hungary and Czechoslovakia. Sometimes messages in very small writing, or passages from the Bible are etched into the pattern.

In Lithuania there is a tradition of making 'look inside' eggs which takes an equally long time. Just like our chocolate eggs these artificial eggs are large and hollow but they are all in one piece with a small hole at each end. Inside, modelled in fondant, is a whole landscape with tiny trees and bushes, hills, rabbits and chickens.

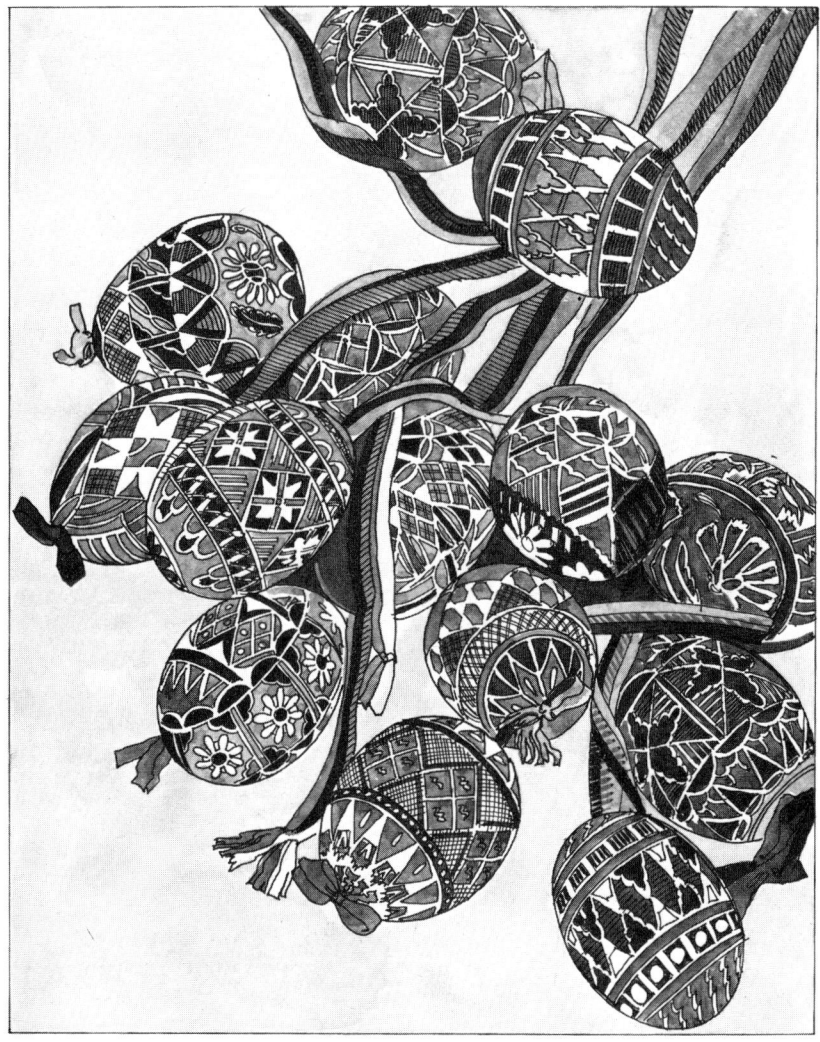

Decorated Easter eggs

These are preparations for Easter day. But just occasionally the Easter celebrations themselves begin on Easter Eve. This is especially true in Sicily, for example, where traditionally the Resurrection has always been celebrated on the Saturday. The Sicilians say that as they are nearer to Palestine than the rest of Italy they heard about the Resurrection a day earlier than anyone else. Other Italians say that the trouble with the Sicilians is that they are always so fond of merrymaking that they just can't put up with the seriousness of Lent and the sorrow of Good Friday for a moment longer.

In Britain too there are some places where Easter begins early. At Barrow in Furness there is an old tradition that the Furness Morris Men perform an old mummers' play on Easter Saturday and Easter Monday. The play itself tells of a battle between St George and a host of odd characters with names like Bold Hector, the King of Egypt, Tosspot and the Bold Slasher.

Bacup Nutters Dance

At Bacup, in Lancashire, Easter Saturday is the occasion for the performance of the Nutters' Dance. Eight men with blackened faces, wearing white caps, black breeches, red and white shirts, white stockings and decorated wooden clogs, dance through the town. As they go they clap the 'nuts', which are the wooden discs from the tops of cotton bobbins used in weaving. These they attach to their waists, hands and knees.

It is hard to say just how or why some of these customs began. Some of them are more a celebration of spring than of the Christian Resurrection and show that the old ways of two thousand years ago have never really died out.

Easter day
In parts of northern Europe Easter day begins at nightfall on Saturday with bonfires, around which there is singing and dancing. In the Hartz Mountains of Germany giant wooden wheels with straw tied to the spokes are set alight and rolled down the slopes. The fields where they come to rest are considered to be lucky and the farmer who owns them will have good crops. This is still a spring festival but as the night passes the festival becomes more and more a Christian celebration.

The first Easter story tells how Mary Magdalene set out 'before it was yet light', and this is remembered in many parts of the world. In some parts of Africa it is customary for young women, dressed in white, to go round the houses singing Easter hymns so that people awake to the good news that Christ is risen.

In parts of America many people spend the whole night together waiting for the sunrise. America is a huge continent and it is daylight in the east five hours before the sun rises on the West coast. The first to greet the sun on Easter morning are the people who gather on Cadillac Mountain in Maine. At the town of Lawton in Oklahoma thousands of worshippers watch a six-hour night-time pageant about the life of Jesus. It ends with the Resurrection scene just as dawn breaks over the mountain top. Many similar services are held across the U.S.A. including one in the famous Hollywood Bowl.

Hollywood Bowl

These American practices are a revival of a tradition that has been going on in the Church in Greece and Russia for nearly two thousand years. For the Eastern Orthodox Church there is no festival like Easter. The service begins on the stroke of midnight. The church is in total darkness as a priest comes out from a door in the sanctuary at the front. He holds a single lighted candle, the only light in the building. His voice breaks the silence. 'Come, ye,' he calls. 'Come and partake of the never-setting light and glorify Christ, who is risen from the dead.'

The members of the congregation come forward one by one. Each holds a candle which is lit from the priest's candle and then passed on to a neighbour, until the whole church is ablaze with flickering light. The priest leads the way out of the church. Once outside he reads the Easter story from the Gospel. As he finishes he chants, 'Christos anesti' (Christ is risen). The congregation take up the chant and reply, 'He is risen indeed.' In some communist countries where attempts have been made to do away with Christianity this ceremony in the street, even in the middle of Moscow, has become a yearly act of witness. Many have been put in prison for doing it.

In England midnight services are not very common at Easter (although see Chapter 3 on Easter vigil). They are more associated with Christmas. Often the first indication of Easter day is the noise of bells from church towers. Traditionally they were kept silent throughout Lent, though this is not done today. On Good Friday a single, muffled bell is sometimes tolled as at a funeral. But on Easter morning they ring out in peal after peal with all the energy that the bellringers can muster.

Easter is a morning festival. It is usually at breakfast that the presents of Easter eggs and other things are given and it is in the morning that the main church services are held. Often there are more people in church that morning than at any other time of the year. It is customary too in some churches for the Easter offering to be given to the priest, the only time of the year that this happens.

The afternoon of Easter day is traditionally taken up with outdoor activities of a type when people meet together. The springtime side of Easter comes to the fore again. It is as if this day marks the end of being shut up indoors. Life out of doors, which will go on through the summer, begins again. It is often a time for new clothes to mark the change of seasons but the custom also goes back to the religious habits of the past when people often deliberately wore old clothes during Lent or even covered themselves and their garments in ashes (see the book *Shrove Tuesday and Ash Wednesday* in this series).

Easter Sunday afternoon is the time of the Easter parade, the showing off of the Easter bonnets. Perhaps the best known parade nowadays is the one held in Battersea Park, London. In

Victorian times most parades were just made up of people strolling up and down the roads but the Battersea Park parade is a real festival procession with decorated floats and bands.

Easter Parade, Battersea Park

Easter Monday

Easter Sunday has a serious side to it. On the following day, Easter Monday, very little is taken seriously. It is here that we see the two sides of celebrating spring and celebrating the Resurrection coming together in one great day of fun and festivity. In Britain in particular it has been a holiday for hundreds of years — a day of fairs and races, hunting and sports meetings, open-air dancing and processions. There is probably more variety than on any other holiday. There are hundreds of different local traditions. Unfortunately, there is room here to deal with only one of the more unusual Easter Monday celebrations, Hare Pie Scramble and Bottle Kicking at Hallaton in Leicestershire.

The story which is told to explain the custom is that many centuries ago a local lady crossing a field was chased by a bull.

Hallaton Hare Pie. The bottles can be seen in the background

She was only saved from being gored to death when a hare ran across the path of the bull causing it to hesitate. In gratitude the woman gave some land to the church on condition that the rector of the parish should distribute two hare pies to the parishioners every year. Making hare pie seems a strange way of showing gratitude to hares, but as we shall see in a later chapter, hares have been associated with Easter for many centuries and there is probably much more behind this particular event than this simple story suggests.

Nowadays small pieces of pie are thrown to the crowd which gathers on a mound known as Hare Pie Bank, just outside the village. There is a scramble to get a portion of the pie and the ceremony is accompanied by much eating and drinking.

The 'bottles' which are kicked are not bottles at all but beer barrels. There are three barrels — two full and one empty. One of the full barrels is placed on top of the mound. The men of Hallaton and the next village of Medbourne face one another. At a given signal each team tries to get the barrel back to its own village. The winners drink the beer. Then they start again but to make it easier the second time round, the empty barrel is used, although the winners take possession of the third barrel, which is full!

Are there any similar local customs near where you live, or were there in the past? What have any such customs got to do with the Easter story?

2

Stories at Easter

For Christians the Easter stories are the stories of how Jesus rose from the dead and showed himself to his followers.

But the word 'Easter' is not a Christian word at all. It comes from the name of a pagan goddess Eostre or Eastre. Her name meant 'the dawn' so that her festival, which took place every spring, was also about light and waking up to new life.

It was probably the great Christian Saint Bede (A.D. 673–735) from Jarrow in the north-east of England who first joined the two festivals together. It was one way of converting the pagans to Christianity. The name 'Easter' was kept but it was the risen Christ who was worshipped. As we see, however, old customs die hard and some of the symbols of our modern Easter probably come from Eostre's festival even if they have long since been given Christian meanings.

The Christian stories of the Resurrection are told over and over again at Easter. They are to be found at the end of the four Gospels. The Gospels of Luke and John tell the stories in much more detail than the other two. You should read these stories as they are told in the Bible. They appear in the following Gospels: Matthew 28; Mark 16; Luke 24; and John 20, 21.

There are six different stories although one of them is really about the Ascension, when Jesus finally left his followers. Here we shall only look at the other five. There are differences in the way of the Gospel writers relate the happenings and it must be said that there is something mysterious about the stories they tell. We should remember that the disciples could not fully understand events themselves. They were dazed and bewildered. In putting these stories down they were telling of what went on inside their heads as much as what was happening outside.

One thing does seem certain. At the beginning of these incidents all the disciples were convinced that Jesus was dead. At the end the same disciples were quite sure that he was alive and that they had seen him — even though at first they had refused to believe it. We know that many of them spent the rest of their lives convincing others. If they had not done so there would be no Christian Church today.

Let us look at the five stories separately:

The appearance of Jesus to Mary (and other women):
(Matthew 28: 1—10; Mark 16: 1—8; Luke 24: 1—12; John 20; 1—18)

All the Gospel writers agree that the first appearance of Jesus was at dawn on the Sunday morning to a woman, or women, near the tomb. John says that Mary Magdalene was on her own, Luke says she had two others with her. Matthew and Mark say she had only one companion but one says it was Salome and the other says it was a woman called Mary.

There are differences too in how the message was given, whether by one angel, or by two, or by Jesus himself.

But notice also the things that are the same. No one could go to the tomb on the Saturday because it was the Sabbath until dusk. The tradition that it was at first light on the Sunday morning is very strong. So are the details that the stone was already rolled away, that it was the women who were first on the scene, and that the majority of the men refused to believe the story.

The appearance on the Emmaus road:
(Mark 16: 12—13; Luke 24: 13—34)

Only two of the four Gospel writers tell this story and only the account by Luke has any detail. It is about two of the men who refused to believe what had happened to the women at the tomb and to whom Jesus appeared as they travelled to Emmaus, though at first they did not recognize him. Only when they stopped to eat together did they realize it was Jesus as 'he took the bread, and blessed it, and brake, and gave to them' (Compare this story with the one in Luke 22: 19.)

Though darkness had fallen the two men hurried back the twenty kilometres to Jerusalem. The other disciples had locked themselves in and the two had some difficulty in getting them to open the door. Even when they entered they found it hard to explain what had happened. They were as certain as the women that Jesus was alive but were unable to convince their friends.

The appearance in the upper room:
(Mark 16: 14—15.; Luke 24: 36—49; John 20: 19—25)

The two men from Emmaus were still trying to convince their friends that they had seen Jesus when suddenly, there he was in the room, though the door was shut and barred. Jesus showed them the wounds in his hands, feet and side. He spoke the Jewish greeting 'Shalom' (Peace be with you) and asked for something to eat. Frightened and puzzled the disciples offered Jesus some cooked fish. And then, as suddenly as he had come, he was gone again. After this experience all the disciples except one believed that Jesus was alive. The exception was Thomas. He was not with the other disciples at the time Jesus appeared and he refused to believe the story until he had some proof.

The appearance to doubting Thomas:
(John 20: 26—31)

It was eight days later that Jesus appeared again. This time Thomas was there and the story tells how Jesus allowed himself to be touched so that Thomas could have the proof he wanted. He also warned him that not everyone can have proof like this and then he disappeared again. Now all the close followers of Jesus believed that he had risen from the dead.

A dramatic interpretation of the Resurrection by Gustave Doré

The appearance at Galilee:
(John 21: 1—25)

Only John's Gospel tells of a final appearance to the disciples who had gone back to Galilee to take up their work as fishermen again. In many details it is just like the story of the first time that Jesus called on these disciples to follow him. (read Luke 5: 2—11).

It is as if the whole story was to begin all over again and in a way this is just what happened. These fishermen did give up their jobs and their homes and they did spend the rest of their lives preaching about the risen Jesus. That is how the Christian Church began to spread, and has continued to grow down to the present day.

Just how much detail in these stories went on in the heads of the disciples and just how much happened exactly as the stories say, we shall never know. These stories are like poems. For Christians they tell the great, central truth of their faith — Christ is risen. The Resurrection came on a Sunday, which is why, right from the start, the disciples changed their sabbath day from the Jewish Saturday in order to celebrate it. The first disciples did not find the Resurrection easy to believe at first either. They could never fully explain it. All they could do was to celebrate it.

This has been the experience of countless men and women over centuries. They have, like the disciples, become convinced that Christ is risen and they have tried to express their feelings in music and poetry and paintings. They express it in festival too — in the great annual festival of Easter, when these stories are told again and again.

3

Symbols of Easter

When Saint Bede converted the festival of Eostre into the festival of Christ's Resurrection many of the old symbols became converted as well. It is perfectly true to say that many of the symbols of Easter are pagan but Christians see in them meanings belonging to their own Resurrection stories. Let us look at a few examples.

Laurel Laurel is an evergreen shrub with a very interesting history. For centuries people have thought of it as an emblem of leadership and victory. The Greeks gave a wreath of laurel to victorious athletes and in the days of the Roman Empire army leaders who have been successful in battle had garlands of laurel placed on their heads.

Nowadays laurel is sometimes used to decorate churches at Easter time. As an evergreen it shows that life goes on through the cold darkness of winter. But the old association is also there. It is a symbol of Christ the victor who has conquered death.

Eggs The making of chocolate eggs is a new custom, but for thousands of years, even before the time of Jesus, people have given eggs to one another as gifts in the spring. They are a sign of new life which is just about to break out. For Christians they quickly came to have a special meaning. Eggs look dead but they contain life. The shell has the shape of a cave-like tomb in which Jesus was buried. On Easter morning the rolling away of the stone was like the breaking of an egg.

In the Middle Ages it was the custom not to eat eggs during Lent. The custom of boiled eggs for breakfast on Easter morning still goes on. For a long time it was literally a breaking of the fast.

The Chick It is not difficult to see why the chick has also become a symbol of Easter. It is the chick which breaks out of the shell as Jesus broke out of the tomb. From the egg comes new life. The Easter chick is small, yellow and fluffy but it quickly grows into the large, brown hen which will lay the eggs from which other chicks will come. And so the cycle of life goes on giving rise to the old question 'Which came first, the chicken or the egg?'.

The Easter bunny In some countries it is said that the Easter bunny brings Easter eggs and children make nests for it in the garden. However, the use of young rabbits as a symbol for Easter today is probably based on a mistake. As we have already seen in the story of the Easter celebrations at Hallaton, it was the hare which was associated with Easter. Almost certainly the hare was used as a sacrifice to Eostre.

As well as these symbols there are others which are probably entirely Christian in their origins and which you will find in many churches at Easter time:

The paschal candle At Easter time in many churches there is a special, very large candle known as the paschal candle. (Paschal is simply another name for Easter. It comes from the Hebrew word *pesach,* or Passover. It was at the time of the Jewish Passover that the events of the first Christian Easter took place.) The paschal candle is large because it has to burn for forty days, from Easter until Ascension Day. Nowadays it is possible to make slow-burning candles but in the past some

A sepulchre built into a church wall

paschal candles were huge. In the Middle Ages the paschal candle in Durham Cathedral was square in shape and went up to within a man's height of the roof. The Gospels tell us that Jesus was the Light of the World. The flame of the candle is a reminder of this and it is a symbol of Jesus showing himself to the disciples during those forty days.

Easter sepulchres An Easter sepulchre is a model of Jesus' tomb. In some old churches a permanent sepulchre was built into the wall and carved with Easter scenes.

Elsewhere they are made of wood, richly carved and decorated. They are sometimes used as part of the Easter services. In some churches the clergy act out the visit to the tomb by Mary, Peter and John to discover again that Christ has risen. In others it is the place of the Easter vigil, the waiting

An Easter garden

through the night for Easter to dawn. In every Roman Catholic church this begins at ten o'clock on the night of Easter eve.

Easter gardens   A more modern custom is the making of an Easter garden to look like the garden in which Jesus' body was laid. These can often be found in schools and homes as well as churches and are made out of mosses and small spring flowers.

In the garden is a miniature sepulchre (a tomb which was either a natural cave or was cut into a hillside). By its side is a large stone, representing the stone which was rolled away to show the empty tomb. Sometimes figures of Peter, John and Mary Magdalene are placed by the tomb.

In the background there is a hill. On it stand three empty crosses, a reminder of the events of Good Friday.

These are the symbols you can see with your eyes. Each one forms only a small part of the Easter celebrations in Christian churches all over the world. There are other symbols of sound and movement. To appreciate them it is perhaps necessary to go into a church on Easter morning, to hear the singing of the Easter hymns and to see the drama of the first Easter morning acted out in many different ways.

4

The Meaning of Easter

As we have seen, it is often difficult to find the real meaning behind festivities such as Easter. The origins of certain activities are obvious while others might not be so clear. Often there may be more than one meaning, with an important message hidden within a simple story. Sometimes the stories themselves may contain different meanings.

So it is with Easter. At one level it is all about the coming of spring, rejoicing because things which seemed dead are coming to life again. At another level it is, for Christians, about the Resurrection of Christ, the conquering of death for all time.

Both are saying that life is stronger than death. While one looks at that idea in the world of nature, the other looks at it as it affects man and his place in the universe. All these ideas are brought together in the one great mixture we call a festival. Hare Pie Scramble and the Resurrection stories all go together. Perhaps we can see the two extremes in the way we fix the date of Easter and the way the New Testament talks about it.

The dating of Easter
Although we know that the events of the first Christian Easter took place at Passover time (see the book in this series *Passover*), Christians in Europe and America still celebrate the

festival according to the phases of the sun and the moon. The spring (or vernal) equinox takes place on 21 March. The word 'equinox' simply means 'equal night'. It is the day on which the sun is directly over the Equator, where there will be twelve hours of light and twelve hours of darkness. In other words the sun, which during winter has been over the southern hemisphere, is coming back to the north.

Easter day comes some time after the equinox; just when, depends on the moon. There must be one full moon after the equinox, then Easter Sunday is the first Sunday after that. This means that Easter day can be on any date between 22 March and 25 April.

There are many people today who want Easter to be on the same date every year. Christians have no real objections because the present way of dating belongs to Eostre rather than to the New Testament.

What the New Testament says about Easter

We have seen how the first disciples tried to tell the story of what happened to them after Jesus had been crucified. Other Christians, when they had had a lot of time to think about it, tried to write down what it all meant.

When St Paul was writing to the church at Corinth he knew that there was an argument going on about whether the Resurrection of Christ was important or not. He had no doubts. He wrote: 'If Christ has not been raised then our preaching is in vain and your faith is in vain. If Christ has not been raised your faith is futile.' (1 Corinthians 15: 14, 17.)

Although the date of Easter is decided by the sun and the moon the dates of other festivals for Christians depend on Easter. Everything revolves around that and the event it celebrates. The power of whatever happened on that first Easter morning began the worship of Christ as God, which started a new religion and changed the world. For Christians it is the central point of history.

Towards the end of his life St Paul tried to say just what it all meant to Christians. In one of his most famous pieces of writing he wrote:

Is it Christ Jesus, who died, yes, who was raised from the dead, who is at the right hand of God, who shall intercede for us? Who shall separate us from the love of Christ? Shall tribulation, or distress, or persecution, or famine, or nakedness, or peril, or the sword?

No, in all these things we are more than conquerors through him who loved us. For I am sure that neither death nor life, nor angels, nor principalities, nor things present, nor things to come, nor powers, nor height, nor depth, nor anything else in all creation, will be able to separate us from the love of God in Christ Jesus our Lord.
(Romans 8: 33—39)

But perhaps even St Paul could not say it all in words. That is why Christians still celebrate this festival. To express what they feel they need to use all the senses, sight, smell, taste and touch, as well as sound and when they do use their voices at Easter the most common cry is simply 'Alleluia! — praise be to God'. There is more meaning yet to be discovered to this greatest of all mysteries.

THINGS TO DO

1 Make your own Easter egg decorations either on real egg shells, or, if that is not possible, on paper.
2 Find out as much as you can about morris dancers and what some of their dances might be about. Say why you think that the morris men start their dancing season at Easter time.
3 Look through a hymn-book and find Easter hymns. Learn to play or sing the melody of one you have not seen before.
4 Write your own Easter carol.
5 Make an 'Easter bonnet' out of bits and pieces. Organize a parade and ask someone to be the judge.
6 Write an imaginative story which begins with words, 'The hare stood all alone in the middle of the field. There was no one in sight. Not a sound could be heard. Suddenly. . .'
7 Find out all you can about local Easter customs. Your public library might be able to help.
8 Read the Easter stories in a modern version of the Bible, using the references given in Chapter 2.
9 Find out all you can from an encyclopaedia about Bede and Eostre. Also look up information on Adonis.
10 Write one of the Easter stories in your own words as if you were one of the women visiting the tomb or one of the men in the other stories. Tell what you feel as well as what you see and hear.
11 Make a collage or a painting using some or all of the symbols mentioned in Chapter 3.

12 Make a paschal candle for your own room or classroom. Light it for a short time every day between Easter and Ascension Day.
13 Make an Easter garden as a class or group project.
14 Make a frieze for the classroom wall putting in as many of the stories, activities and symbols associated with Easter as you can.
15 Draw a diagram to show the meaning of spring or vernal equinox.
16 Try and get hold of a record of Handel's *Messiah* and listen to the 'Hallelujah Chorus'. Discuss what the words and music together are attempting to say about Easter.
17 Compose, or write the words for a song to be part of a rock musical. The title of the song could be *Easter's the Time for a Big Celebration*.
18 Write out the words of one of the statements of St Paul given in Chapter 4, perhaps as an illuminated manuscript. Then learn the words by heart.
19 Write an essay on 'Why festivals are to be celebrated not just learned about', using Easter as an example.

MATERIAL FOR TEACHERS

Useful addresses

Christian Education Movement
2 Chester House
Pages Lane
London N10 1PR

National Society
23 Kensington Square
London W8

Your local churches often provide the best examples of Easter celebrations, but remember that clergy and ministers are very busy and do not have time to write lots of replies to letters. Invite them to school to talk about Easter preparations, or go to church on Easter day.

Books to read about Easter

Bradling, Redvers. *Festive Occasions in the Primary School.* Ward Lock, 1980.
Bull, Norman J. *Festivals and Customs.* A. Wheaton & Co. Ltd, 1979.
Gascoigne, Margaret. *Discovering English Customs and Traditions.* Shire Publications, 1976.
Hunt, P. J. *What to Look for Inside a Church.* Ladybird, 1972.
———. *What to Look for Outside a Church.* Ladybird, 1972.
Lord, P. S. *Easter the World Over.* Chilton Book Co.
Newall, V. *An Egg at Easter.* Routledge & Kegan Paul (for Secondary pupils and teachers only).
Pearson, N. F. *Stories of Special Days and Customs.* Ladybird, 1972.
Tompkins, Sue. *Christian Objects.* Christian Education Movement.
Vaughan, Jenny. *The Easter Book* MacDonald Educational.

Workcards

Rankin, John. *Looking at Festivals.* Lutterworth.

Assembly books on festivals

Green, Victor. *Festivals and Saints' Days.* Blandford.
Purton, Rowland. *Festivals and Celebrations.* Blackwell, 1979.
Smith, Harry. *Assemblies.* Heinemann, 1981.
also: *Together for Festivals.* Church Information Office.